PAUL ROBESON

PAUL ROBESON

By Eloise Greenfield
Illustrated by George Ford

Thomas Y. Crowell

New York

CROWELL BIOGRAPHIES
Edited by Susan Bartlett Weber

JANE ADDAMS *by Gail Faithfull Keller*

MARIAN ANDERSON *by Tobi Tobias*

LEONARD BERNSTEIN *by Molly Cone*

MARTHA BERRY *by Mary Kay Phelan*

WILT CHAMBERLAIN *by Kenneth Rudeen*

RAY CHARLES *by Sharon Bell Mathis*

CESAR CHAVEZ *by Ruth Franchere*

SAMUEL CLEMENS
by Charles Michael Daugherty

ROBERTO CLEMENTE *by Kenneth Rudeen*

CHARLES DREW *by Roland Bertol*

FANNIE LOU HAMER *by June Jordan*

LANGSTON HUGHES, AMERICAN POET
by Alice Walker

JAMES WELDON JOHNSON
by Ophelia Settle Egypt

FIORELLO LA GUARDIA
by Mervyn Kaufman

THE MAYO BROTHERS *by Jane Goodsell*

ARTHUR MITCHELL *by Tobi Tobias*

JOHN MUIR *by Charles P. Graves*

JESSE OWENS *by Mervyn Kaufman*

GORDON PARKS *by Midge Turk*

ROSA PARKS *by Eloise Greenfield*

THE RINGLING BROTHERS *by Molly Cone*

PAUL ROBESON *by Eloise Greenfield*

JACKIE ROBINSON *by Kenneth Rudeen*

ELEANOR ROOSEVELT *by Jane Goodsell*

MARIA TALLCHIEF *by Tobi Tobias*

JIM THORPE *by Thomas Fall*

THE WRIGHT BROTHERS
by Ruth Franchere

MALCOLM X *by Arnold Adoff*

Library of Congress Cataloging in Publication Data. Greenfield, Eloise. Paul Robeson. SUMMARY: A biography of the black man who became a famous singer, actor, and spokesman for equal rights for his people. 1. Robeson, Paul, 1898- —Juv. lit. [1. Robeson, Paul, 1898-   2. Singers, American. 3. Negroes—Biography] I. Ford, George, fl. illus. II. Title. E185.97.R642 790.2'0924 [B] [92] 74-13663 ISBN 0-690-00552-0 ISBN 0-690-00660-8 (lib. bdg.)

5   6   7   8   9   10

PAUL ROBESON

When William D. Robeson was a boy, he was a slave on a plantation in North Carolina. He hated being a slave. He hated it so much that when he was fifteen years old, he did a very dangerous thing.

He ran away.

If he had been caught, the slaveowner would have beaten him with a whip or killed him. But William Robeson was determined to be free.

He escaped to the North, where he went to school. After he graduated from college, he married Maria Louisa Bustill and became pastor of the Witherspoon Street Presbyterian Church in Princeton, New Jersey.

Princeton was a small town built around a big university. The university was for white students. White people who lived in the town often went to meetings and parties at the university. Black people went to meetings and parties at Reverend Robeson's church.

On April 9, 1898, in the parsonage of the church, the youngest child of Reverend and Mrs. Robeson was born. They named him Paul Leroy Robeson.

Reverend Robeson was fifty-three years old, not a young man, when Paul was born. Mrs. Robeson was sickly and almost blind. Even with her thick glasses, she still could not see very well. But Paul's mother and father and sister and three brothers were all very happy to welcome the new baby into the family.

Paul was still a baby when his father lost his position at the church because of an argument among the members. This was a hard blow for Reverend Robeson, but in his quiet, strong way, he went about finding a new way to support his family. He bought a horse named Bess and a wagon, and people who lived in Princeton paid him to take away the ashes from their coal furnaces.

When Paul was old enough, he often watched Bess pull the wagon into the back yard so that his father could dump the ashes. Paul and Bess became good friends.

Sometimes Reverend Robeson or Paul's brother, Reeve, hitched Bess to a large carriage and drove passengers where they wanted to go. Some of the passengers were students from Princeton University. More than once, Reeve fought these students for making insulting remarks about black people.

Reeve taught Paul that he should always
stand up for his rights. Paul admired Reeve,
Bill, Marian, and Ben, and they loved their
little brother. Paul was big for his age, and the
boys taught him to play football. Sometimes,

4

in the evenings after dinner, they sang. Paul was happiest when Bill was home on vacation from college and the whole family could be together.

But when Paul was six years old, a tragic accident upset the family's happiness. One day when his mother was cleaning the house, she bumped into the coal stove that kept the house warm. A hot coal fell on her long dress, setting it on fire, and she was burned to death.

At first Paul could not believe that his mother was really dead. But later he knew it was true because he missed her so much. Relatives and friends who lived nearby invited the younger Robeson children to their homes for dinner, or to spend days at a time. Like the Robesons, they didn't have much money. But they were glad to share their homes. They were full of love for the children and tried to make them feel better.

Paul grew very close to his father. They played checkers together and read together. His father taught him to recite and helped him study his homework.

Paul liked school. Once in a while a teacher had to spank him for not behaving, but he always did his work. He had learned from his father the importance of always doing his best.

He learned many other things by watching and listening to his father. He learned to love words—written words and spoken words. He learned to be proud of being black. He learned that people should do the things they really believe in.

A few years after Mrs. Robeson's death, Reverend Robeson again became pastor of a church. The church was in Westfield, near Princeton. Later he had a church in Somerville, also near Princeton.

Paul was proud when he sat in church and listened to his father's sermons. He could see that the words meant a lot to the members of the church. They liked what Reverend Robeson was saying and they liked the rhythm of his deep bass voice.

Paul sang in the church choir. He loved music, especially the black music called Spirituals. Spirituals are religious songs. They are a mixture of the music that slaves had known in Africa and the music and words they added to it after they were kidnapped to America.

At Somerville High School, Paul sang the
solos in the glee club. He liked to sing, and he
sang well. But he didn't think he would want

8

to make his living as a singer when he grew up.

He knew he didn't want to be an actor. One year his school gave a performance of *Othello,* a play written almost four hundred years ago by William Shakespeare. Paul played the part of an African general. It was the main part, and he was so nervous that he promised himself he would never try acting again.

Years later Paul would be famous all over the world for his great acting in *Othello* and other plays, and for his singing. But he did not know that then.

Summers Paul went to Rhode Island with Ben. He worked in the kitchen of a hotel for rich people, and Ben worked as a waiter.

At school, Paul not only acted and sang, he played football, baseball, and basketball. He was on the track team. He made speeches as a member of the debating club. Still he found time for study, and he graduated with honors.

He won a four-year scholarship to Rutgers College, which is now Rutgers University. He would not have to pay to go to college.

Paul was very tall now, big-boned and broad-shouldered. He was a dark, proud, and rather quiet young man looking forward to college.

At Rutgers, there was only one other black student. There had not been many black students at the high school either, and Paul had had problems with some of the white students and teachers. But worse things happened at Rutgers.

Paul was not allowed to sing in the glee club because there were parties after the musical programs that no black person could attend.

He tried out for football, but the other players did not want a black student on the team. On the first day that the coach sent them out on the field to practice, one player smashed Paul in the face with his fist. Paul fell down and the other players jumped on him and punched him with their fists and knees and elbows.

Paul went home with a broken nose. His shoulder had been knocked out of place, and he had scratches and bruises all over his body. He stayed in bed ten days. He was hurting and he was thinking.

He was thinking about whether or not he wanted to try out for the team again. He hated being hurt. But he didn't want to be a quitter.

Also, he knew that if he made the team, it would give hope to other young black athletes.

Paul went back to practice determined to make it. He knew that he was big and strong and that he had been the star player on his high school team. If the other boys played fair, he could show the coach what he could do.

On the first play, Paul made a tackle, pulling the boy carrying the ball down with him. Another player ran over, lifted his foot, and stamped on Paul's hand. The cleats on the bottom of his football shoes dragged all the fingernails off Paul's fingers.

Paul was mad. The pain and the unfairness made him madder than he had ever been. He picked up one of the players and lifted him up over his head. Just as he started to slam the boy to the ground, the coach ran up to him.

''Paul, you're on the team!'' he yelled. ''I'm picking you for the team!''

Paul put the boy down.

The Rutgers team was lucky to have Paul. He became its hero. Newspapers wrote about Paul Robeson, the tall black athlete. They told how he stopped the players trying to run past him with the ball. They told how he reached up with his long arms to snatch the ball out of the air and take it for a touchdown. They told how he hurled his body against anybody who tried to stop a Rutgers teammate.

Crowds came to see "Big Robey," and almost always in the crowd was Reverend Robeson, proudly watching his son.

Paul and his father were still close. Whenever Paul went home for a weekend, they spent many hours together. Together they planned Paul's future.

Paul had decided to be a lawyer, and his father was happy about it. But Reverend Robeson died near the end of Paul's third year of college. Paul was sad when he returned to Rutgers for his last year. His father would not be in the audience when he graduated.

Graduation day came in 1919 when Paul was twenty-one years old. He had won many honors in college. He had been elected to Phi Beta Kappa, a group of outstanding students. He had been a debating champion. He had won awards in four sports. Twice, he had been named All-American End. This meant that Paul was one of the best college athletes in the United States.

As the student with the best grades in the

whole graduating class, Paul was chosen to make the farewell speech. From the stage, he said good-bye to Rutgers for himself and his classmates.

The following year Paul moved to New York City to attend the Columbia University Law School. Weekends he played professional football to earn money. Most of his free time was spent in Harlem, where he lived. Harlem is the part of New York where many black people live and work. Paul saw plays at the Lafayette Theater. He visited friends and went to parties.

At the parties people loved to hear him sing. A friend would play the piano and Paul would sing Spirituals. He sang about slaves being a long way from home and about slave children riding the train to freedom. The room would grow very quiet as people listened to the sound of Paul's deep, throbbing voice.

Paul's speaking voice was as rich and deep-toned as his singing voice. When the Harlem Young Women's Christian Association decided to give a play, Paul's friends asked him to take a part in it.

Paul played the main part, but this time he wasn't as nervous as he had been in high school. Many people told him that he was a good actor. But he did not take it seriously. He wanted to be a lawyer.

At Columbia University, where he was studying hard, something wonderful happened to Paul. He met Eslanda Goode, who was studying science there. Her friends called her Essie. Paul and Essie fell in love, and one summer day they were married.

The next summer Paul was invited to England, across the Atlantic Ocean. A theater company needed a black actor, and someone who had seen Paul act suggested him for the job.

Paul and Essie went. They enjoyed traveling
to the different towns and cities of England.
While there, they met Lawrence Brown, who
became a good friend.

Lawrence Brown was a pianist. He loved Spirituals as much as Paul did. He not only played them on the piano, he arranged them. He put the notes in order and wrote them on music paper.

At the end of the summer, the Robesons returned to New York so that Paul could finish school.

Paul was very happy when he became a lawyer. Now he would be able to go into court and help people in trouble. But it was hard for a black lawyer, especially a new one, to find work.

He finally got a job with a white law firm, but some members of the firm refused to work with a black lawyer. After a few weeks, Paul left.

Now he was out of a job. But people were asking him to be in their plays. They wanted to pay Paul Robeson for his talent. More and more, he appeared on the stage. In some of the plays, he both acted and sang.

Paul had never taken acting or singing lessons. He acted by making himself feel the way he thought the character would feel. He spent hours reading his part over and over. Sometimes he sat in a quiet place and thought about it.

Paul also appeared on musical programs called concerts. Lawrence Brown came to New York, and he and Paul gave a concert of all black music. A concert with one person singing Spirituals and other black songs was a new idea. Many people wanted to hear. They filled all the seats at the theater, and some people even stood up.

Lawrence Brown played the piano and Paul sang. Paul made his voice sometimes loud, sometimes soft, sometimes happy, sometimes sad. Some notes he chopped off and some he

held a long, long time. Every note had to be just right. He wanted the audience to feel what he felt about black music.

At the end of the concert, the audience cheered and yelled for more. They did not want the concert to end.

Paul Robeson and Lawrence Brown became a famous team. For many years, they traveled all over the United States and to other parts of the world to give concerts. They went to Africa, France, the West Indies, Russia, England, and many other places. Paul not only sang at concerts, he made records and he appeared in plays and movies and on the radio.

Paul was in England when his son was born. He and Essie named the baby Paul, Jr. Sometimes the baby traveled with them.

Paul Robeson liked meeting and talking with the people of different countries. He learned their languages and sang their songs.

He especially loved Africa—the people and languages, the stories and poetry, the music and art. Because he was black, he felt very close to Africa.

Everywhere he went, crowds came to see him. Teachers brought their classes to see him as Othello. People gave parties for him and gave him awards. Newspapers and magazines wrote about his ability to walk and talk and look like the characters he played. They wrote about his ability to make audiences cry or feel good.

But Paul could not always enjoy these things. He saw many problems that made him sad and worried and angry.

He saw that some countries were fighting each other. He saw that black people were not treated fairly. He saw that many African countries were ruled by white governments. In many parts of the world he met people who

did not have enough money to buy food and warm clothes and have a nice place to live. Paul could not be happy unless he tried to help.

He began to make speeches at his concerts.

After he sang, he talked. He talked about black freedom, and good jobs for all people, and peace. Audiences listened when he talked. Many people wanted to hear what he had to say.

But not everybody.

Not everybody liked what he was saying. Some people did not want him to talk about problems. But Paul had to do what he believed was right. He often thought of his father. He wanted to be as strong and as true to his beliefs as his father had been. He not only continued to speak out, he worked too.

He marched with signs in front of theaters where black people had to sit in special seats. He marched in front of the offices of baseball teams that would not hire black ballplayers. He went to see the President of the United States to protest the killings of black people in the South. He started a newspaper called

Freedom. He helped to start groups who worked for black freedom. He wrote articles for magazines.

Often Paul went to large peace meetings held by Communists. Communists believe in a different kind of government than the one in the United States. Many people do not like Communists. They are afraid they will make the United States a Communist country.

In the 1940's and 1950's, some members of Congress in Washington, D.C., where laws are made, began to punish Communists and their friends. They made them lose their jobs or sent them to jail. The people who wanted Paul Robeson to stop talking about problems began to punish him for having Communist friends.

It became very hard for Paul to find places to perform. Owners of many theaters, concert halls, and radio and television stations would

not allow him to sing or act. Owners of record stores stopped selling his records. Some of them were angry with him, and some were afraid that they would be punished too.

Sometimes, but not very often, Paul could perform in a church or a park. When he did, large audiences came to see him. They came even though they were sometimes attacked by Paul's enemies.

One afternoon Paul gave an outdoor concert near Peekskill, New York. Twenty-five thousand people came to hear him. A much smaller crowd came to try to keep him from singing. They yelled and blew horns during the concert. But Paul kept singing. At the end of the concert, a group of friends formed a bodyguard for Paul. They walked him to his car and saw that he left safely.

Then the real trouble began. Paul's audience was attacked. They were beaten with clubs. Men, women, and children trying to leave in the buses and cars were hit with bricks and bottles and broken glass. Empty cars were turned over.

The attackers were not arrested.

The following year, Paul was told that he could not visit other countries.

"Stop talking and just sing," he was told.

But Paul said, "No." He said that he had the right to both travel and speak. He took his case to court for judges to decide.

While the judges were considering his case, Paul could not leave the United States. But his voice could.

Several times he sang at the line between the United States and Canada. He stood on a stage in the United States on one side of the line. His audience sat in a park in Canada, on the other side of the line.

Once, almost a thousand people went to a concert in England. Paul was not there, but his voice traveled across the Atlantic Ocean by telephone. The last song he sang was "Old Man River." One line in this song says that a man is tired of living and scared of dying. Paul changed this line. He sang, "I must keep fighting until I'm dying."

Paul Robeson kept fighting. He kept fighting for freedom for all people, and he kept fighting for himself. He had to go to court many times to get back his right to travel. Finally, after eight years, he won. He could travel again.

In the years that followed, millions of blacks in America began to feel close to their African heritage. Many of them marched for their rights and for better jobs. Many black singers and actors spoke out for black freedom, as Paul Robeson had.

In April 1973, at Carnegie Hall in New York, twenty famous stars gave a program before a large audience. They were celebrating Paul Robeson's seventy-fifth birthday. He was too sick to attend, but his son came in his place. Paul, Jr., is as close to his father as Paul Robeson was to his.

Paul Robeson has written a book called *Here*

I Stand. It is about his life as a boy and his beliefs as a man. In this book he says, "The glory of my boyhood years was my father."

Paul Robeson, like his father, is determined to be free. He says that although black people cannot yet sing, "Thank God Almighty, we're free at last," they can sing, "Thank God Almighty, we're *moving*!"

THE AUTHOR

Eloise Greenfield was born in Parmele, North Carolina, only a few miles from the place where Paul Robeson's father was a slave. Ms. Greenfield grew up in Washington, D.C., where she lives now with her husband and family. She is the mother of a grown son and a teen-age daughter.

Ms. Greenfield is the author of several books for children. Her short stories and articles have been published in *Black World, Ebony Jr., Scholastic, Scope,* and other magazines. Her Crowell Biography *Rosa Parks,* published in 1973, won the first Carter G. Woodson Award for Social Education.

In 1973 Ms. Greenfield was Writer-in-Residence for the D.C. Commission on the Arts. She has headed both the Adult Fiction and the Children's Literature Divisions of the D.C. Black Writers' Workshop.

THE ARTIST

George Ford shared the Fifth Annual Coretta Scott King Award with author Sharon Bell Mathis for their Crowell Biography *Ray Charles,* published in 1973. Mr. Ford has illustrated more than a score of children's books, many of which have won special recognition. Born in Brooklyn, he spent his childhood there and in the West Indies. He now lives in Harlem, where he works closely with various cultural groups active in the Black community. In 1972 he was elected President of the Council on Interracial Books for Children.